WITCHES

Fly!

abdobooks.com

Published by Abdo Zoom, a division of ABDO, P.O. Box 398166, Minneapolis,
Minnesota 55439. Copyright © 2020 by Abdo Consulting Group, Inc. International
copyrights reserved in all countries. No part of this book may be reproduced in any
form without written permission from the publisher. Fly!™ is a trademark and logo
of Abdo Zoom.

Printed in the United States of America, North Mankato, Minnesota.
102019
012020

THIS BOOK CONTAINS
RECYCLED MATERIALS

Photo Credits: Alamy, AP Images, Everett Collection, iStock, Shutterstock,
©PumpkinSky p17 / CC BY-SA 3.0
Production Contributors: Kenny Abdo, Jennie Forsberg, Grace Hansen
Design Contributors: Dorothy Toth, Neil Klinepier, Pakou Moua

Library of Congress Control Number: 2019941601

Publisher's Cataloging-in-Publication Data

Names: Abdo, Kenny, author.
Title: Witches / by Kenny Abdo
Description: Minneapolis, Minnesota : Abdo Zoom, 2020 | Series: Guidebooks to the
    unexplained | Includes online resources and index.
Identifiers: ISBN 9781532129384 (lib. bdg.) | ISBN 9781644942918 (pbk.) |
    ISBN 9781098220365 (ebook) | ISBN 9781098220853 (Read-to-Me ebook)
Subjects: LCSH: Witches--Juvenile literature. | Spells--Juvenile literature. | Folklore-
    Juvenile literature. | Legends--Juvenile literature. | Magic--Juvenile literature.
Classification: DDC 133.43--dc23

TABLE OF CONTENTS

WITCHES

With mystical powers and steaming **cauldrons**, witches always seem to be brewing something evil.

However, the real history of witches is as dark and deadly as one of their brewed **potions**.

CLASSIFICATION

The word "witch" comes from the Old English word *Wicca*.

Early European Christians feared that witches were true beings of evil. One of the earliest mentions of them is in the Christian Bible. Exodus 22:18 reads, "Thou shalt not suffer a witch to live."

Witches have been described in many
ways throughout history. Sometimes
they are sinister wart-nosed women
who fly over villages on a broom.
Some take the form of menacing
animals like black cats and bats.

DECLASSIFIED

Witch **hysteria** began in Europe
during the mid-1400s. Many
accused witches confessed to wicked
actions, usually after being tortured.

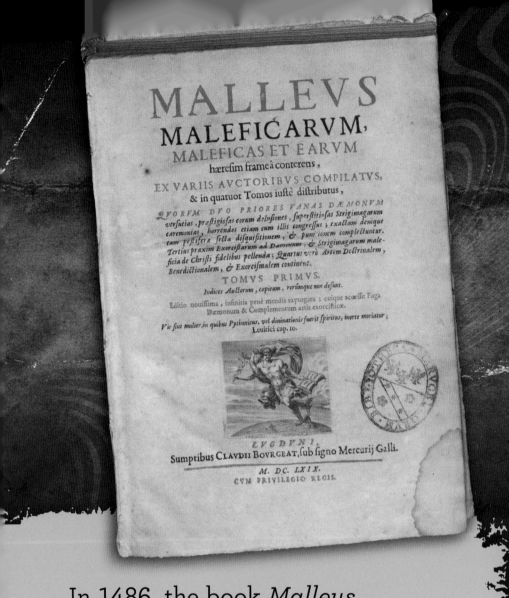

In 1486, the book *Malleus Maleficarum* was published. It was a guide on how to recognize, track, and question witches. It is considered to be what caused witch panic throughout Europe.

Between the years 1500 and 1700, more than 80,000 **alleged** witches were sentenced to death. Most of them were women accused of having a **pact** with the devil.

Mass **hysteria** broke out in Salem, Massachusetts in 1692. Many young girls began to exhibit symptoms of **possession**. More than 150 villagers were accused of using **black magic**. And 18 of them were put to death.

IN MEMORY OF
GRACE WHITE SHERWOOD
1660 — 1740
HEALER OF SICK WITH HERBS
CONVICTED AS A WITCH
SHE SURVIVED VIRGINIA'S ONLY
TRIAL BY DUCKING IN THE
LYNNHAVEN RIVER
JULY 10, 1706
NAME CLEARED BY GOVERNOR
300 YEARS LATER

Grace Sherwood was accused of **hexing** in 1706. The court tied up Sherwood's legs and arms and threw her into water. They believed that if she floated, she was indeed a witch. Sherwood never sank, so she was imprisoned.

Witchcraft is still happening today. You will find Wiccans in places like Africa, the Middle East, South and North America, and Papua New Guinea.

IN MEDIA

Witches have populated every form of media throughout the decades. You'll find them on TV shows like *Wizards of Waverly Place* and *Sabrina the Teenage Witch*. Or on the big screen in popular movies like *Hocus Pocus* and *Harry Potter*.

As with history, witches are either seen as fun old ladies that like to pull pranks or wicked beings who make deals with the devil. Either way, stay far away from their ovens.

GLOSSARY

allege – to claim something was done without proof.

big screen – another name for the movies.

black magic – magic that involves evil spirits, used for evil reasons.

cauldron – a large pot that is used for cooking over an open fire.

hex – to cast a spell of bad luck onto someone.

hysteria – uncontrollable panic among a community.

pact – a strict agreement between two people or a group.

possession – to be out of control of your own body and mind.

potion – a liquid with magical effects.

ONLINE RESOURCES

Booklinks
NONFICTION NETWORK
FREE! ONLINE NONFICTION RESOURCES

To learn more about witches, please visit abdobooklinks.com or scan this QR code. These links are routinely monitored and updated to provide the most current information available.

INDEX